T0276985

THE PHILOSOPHY OF
COFFEE

THE PHILOSOPHY OF
COFFEE

BRIAN WILLIAMS

First published 2018 by
The British Library
96 Euston Road
London NW1 2DB

ISBN 978 0 7123 5230 7
Cataloguing in Publication Data
A catalogue record for this book is available
from the British Library

Designed and typeset by Sandra Friesen
Printed and bound in the Czech Republic by Finidr

CONTENTS

INTRODUCTION

THIS SLIM volume does not set out to be a definitive history of coffee, nor, given its size, does it claim to be an authority on the subject. Rather, consider it an introduction, a brief and (hopefully) entertaining charge through the topic, from coffee's humble origins in northeast Africa over a millennium ago, to what it is today, a global phenomenon that is enjoyed around the world.

It's often said that, after oil, coffee is the second most-traded commodity on the planet. We'll see later that this is not quite true, but coffee is undeniably a commodity of global importance. According to the International Trade Centre, it knocks tea into a cocked hat (the export market for coffee is about seven times that of tea) and ranks up there with other favoured (legal) drugs such as wine and tobacco, and slightly ahead of chocolate.

In the history of human civilisation, however, coffee came very late to the (drinks) party. Compared to wine and beer, which have been around for at least five thousand years, and even tea, which dates back over two thousand years, coffee has barely made it into its second millennium. So how did this late arrival grow, over a comparatively short period of time, to become the global giant of today?

That's the first question this book will seek to answer.

THE ORIGINS OF COFFEE

COMMON CONSENSUS is that coffee originated in the highlands of Ethiopia, its discovery down to a humble goatherd. We have no written evidence for this, just stories passed down through the generations, which, over time, have become the folklore of coffee. A counter-claim is sometimes put forward that Yemen, on the other side of the Red Sea from Ethiopia, is the birthplace of coffee. Despite Yemen's later role in the spread of coffee to the wider world, most experts agree that coffee originated in Ethiopia.

The story was first told in print in 1671 by Antoine Faustus Nairon in one of the earliest surviving treatises devoted to coffee, *De Saluberrima potione Cahue seu Cafe nuncupata Discurscus*. These days, the story is widely known as 'the Legend of Kaldi (and his dancing goats)', and the events it tells are reputed to have taken place anywhere between 800 and 1000 CE. It goes something like this.

Kaldi was a goatherd who noticed that his goats became frisky after eating the red berries from a certain tree. Moreover, the goats were so energised that they couldn't sleep at

KALDI AND HIS DANCING GOATS
THE LEGENDARY DISCOVERY OF THE COFFEE DRINK

night. Intrigued, the curious Kaldi decided to try the beans himself and, as the legend goes, soon joined his goats in their merry dance.

And that, in a nutshell, is how coffee was discovered. Except of course that the story raises far more questions than it answers, the main one being that the goats were eating berries – a far cry from the drink that you and I would recognise as coffee. How did we get from a goatherd (and his goats) eating berries to the drink that we know and love today?

Here accounts differ slightly, but the majority view is that Islam played a key role. According to one version of the legend, Kaldi took the berries to a Sufi monk in a nearby monastery, but the monk, disapproving of their intoxicating effect, threw them onto the fire. Another version has the monk making a drink from the berries, finding it disgusting, and throwing the remaining berries onto the fire. Regardless of the precise motivation, the berries found their way onto the fire, resulting in a delightful aroma being given off. Disgust quickly changed to approval, the monks recovered the (now roasted) beans, and the drink of coffee was born.

In yet another version of the legend, it is the Sufi monk who approached Kaldi, having heard about his energetic antics. According to this version, the monk kept falling asleep in the middle of his prayers and, intrigued by the powers of Kaldi's berries, tried them for himself. They were just as effective on the monk, who subsequently came up with the idea of turning them into a tasty drink, which soon proved popular with his fellow monks.

Whichever version you prefer, the connection has been made between the red berries the goats were feasting on and the drink that we now know as coffee. However, you'd be forgiven for asking what these little red berries have to do with the brown beans that go into making your daily cup of coffee.

Unsurprisingly, the answer is far more complicated than simply throwing the berries on a fire.

WHAT IS COFFEE?

THE LEGEND of Kaldi rather glosses over the whole process of getting from berries on a tree to the drink that we enjoy today. This is in fact a rather involved process, far more complicated that the legend would have us believe.

Going back to first principles, coffee is, in fact, a fruit, which grows on a tree (or bush). The process of going from a ripe coffee cherry (that is, the red berry in the legend) to the finished, roasted bean is very complex. It is certainly more involved than fermenting wine or beer and, compared to coffee, getting from plant to cup when you're talking tea is a doddle, all of which might explain why coffee took so long to be discovered.

Coffee comes from a tree in the botanical family *Coffea,* which grows primarily in the tropical regions at varying altitudes. A typical tree, grown from seed, takes three to five years to mature into a flowering plant, with the flowers maturing once or twice a year into ripe cherries.

Although I use the term coffee *beans*, they are, strictly speaking, *seeds*; the first step, after harvesting the ripe

cherries, is to extract these seeds. While coffee cherries vary in size, all have a very specific structure. First there is the outer skin of the cherry, inside which is the sweet, fruity pulp. This usually contains two hemispherical seeds (except for peaberries, where there is only one). The seeds themselves are wrapped in a thin layer called the silverskin, which in turn is surrounded by a protective layer known as the parchment.

The trick is to strip the seed of these protective coverings (the silverskin, parchment, pulp and outer skin), a technique known as processing or milling. There are three principal methods: washed, natural and pulped natural, each affecting the flavour of the resulting bean. The oldest method, which originated in Ethiopia and is still widely used today, is the natural method. Whole cherries are left to dry in the sun, natural fermentation breaking down the cherry, which is removed (by washing) at the end of the process. Naturally processed coffees tend to exhibit strong, fruity, sweet flavours with plenty of body.

The main alternative is the washed method. Here the outer skin is mechanically removed, before a water-intensive process, which uses up to 20 times the weight of beans in water, strips the pulp from the beans. In contrast to natural coffees, washed coffees are often cleaner-tasting and exhibit more subtle flavours.

The pulped natural method (sometimes called the honey process) combines the two techniques. As in the washed

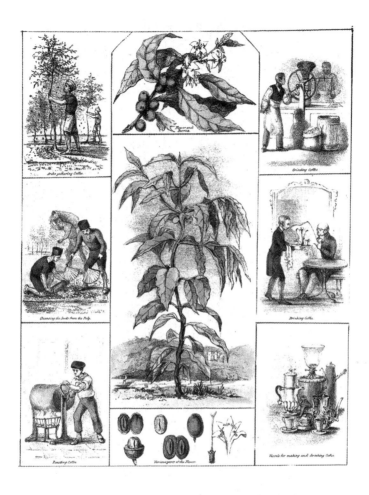

Flower and Berries.

Arabs gathering Coffee.

Grinding Coffee.

Cleansing the Seeds from the Pulp.

Drinking Coffee.

Roasting Coffee.

Various parts of the Flower.

Vessels for making and drinking Coffee.

method, the outer skin is mechanically removed (known as pulping), but the resulting fruit is left to dry, as in the natural method. Typically these coffees have high levels of sweetness, with more acidity than their natural counterparts and more body than washed coffees.

Regardless of the method, it takes at least two weeks to process and then dry the beans before they are sent to a dry mill. Here any remaining parchment and skin is removed, before the resulting green beans, as they are known, are graded and sorted. They are now ready for roasting, or, more usually, exporting in green-bean form. The reason for this is simple: once roasted, coffee quickly loses its freshness; people will argue over exactly how long this takes, but generally speaking, beans should be used within a month of roasting. Green beans, in contrast, retain their freshness for anything up to a year, so they can be shipped by container. Roasted beans, on the other hand, need to be airfreighted.

Finally, there is roasting, the process which produces the familiar brown beans most of us know as coffee. If you've ever stuck your head in a sack of green coffee beans and sniffed hard, you'll have been hit by an intense, vegetal smell. Compare this to the familiar aroma from a bag of coffee beans. This is the result of roasting, the process of applying heat to the green beans. This causes chemical reactions between the acids and sugars in the bean, followed by caramelisation of the sugars, leading to the development of the familiar flavours. There are also physical changes. First the water vapour is driven off (known as first crack, literally a cracking of the beans as water vapour violently escapes). Then, if you roast for long enough, there is the second crack as excess carbon dioxide escapes.

In Kaldi's day, roasting would have been done in a large pan over an open flame, a technique still used in coffee-growing regions around the world (and something you can do at home; I use a wok, but a large frying pan works just as well). These days, drum roasters are more commonly used, a technology that has not changed much in basic principle for about 100 years.

Now all we have to do is make the coffee, but that's for later. In the meantime, how did coffee spread from its discovery in the highlands of Ethiopia to conquer the world? The answer is Islam.

THE WINE OF ISLAM

THE RISE of coffee from an obscure drink in the highlands of Ethiopia to something consumed around the world is inextricably linked with Islam, and, in particular, the Sufi religious orders in Yemen.[1]

As we discovered earlier, the legends behind the discovery of coffee already include a religious aspect, with monks being credited with the actual invention of the drink that we know as coffee. Some have argued that the use of the term 'monks' implies that Christianity, rather than Islam, is behind the discovery of coffee, since Islam has no concept of a monk. Regardless, it is widely accepted that coffee was adopted by the Sufi religious orders in Yemen. Quite when it made the leap from the Ethiopian highlands across the narrow stretch of the Red Sea is lost in history. The earliest documentary evidence of its use in Yemen comes in the early fifteenth century, although it is believed that it was well established before then. However, if the legends of Kaldi are to be believed, and coffee was first discovered between

COFFEE MERCHANTS.

THE CUSTOM OF EXTRACTING A DRINK FROM COFFEE BERRIES IS LOST IN ANTIQUITY—THE BEST COFFEE IN THE WORLD IS PRODUCED ON THE MOUNTAINS OF YEMEN, FROM BEING EXPORTED FROM MOCHA IT IS CALLED MOCHA COFFEE, THE ENGRAVING SHOWS A PARTY OF MERCHANTS ON THEIR WAY TO THE COAST WITH THE PRODUCE OF THEIR COFFEE PLANTATIONS.

800 and 1000 CE, this still leaves a gap in our knowledge of several centuries.

The Sufi orders in Yemen used coffee in their ceremonies. Coffee's role was probably as a stimulant, helping the participants to stay awake, since ceremonies often lasted all night. Coffee may also have helped to produce a euphoric state which aided Sufi attempts to come into more immediate contact with the divine.

Quite what caused the use of coffee to spread beyond the Sufis in Yemen is unclear, but it seems that coffee began its steady march across the Islamic world in the fifteenth and sixteenth centuries. Writing in 1587, the impressively named Abd-al-Kâdir ibn Mohammad al Ansâri al Jazari al Hanbali (al Jazari) produced one of the earliest works about coffee. Al Jazari puts coffee in common use in Yemen by around 1450, and also writes about the first known banning of coffee in Mecca in 1511, which we will come to later. He reinforces the link between coffee and Islam, saying:

> It was drunk in the sacred mosque of Mecca itself ... They drank it every Monday and Friday evening, putting it in a large vessel made of red clay. Their leader ladled it out with a small dipper and gave it to them to drink, passing it to the right.

By the start of the sixteenth century, coffee was also well established in the Mamluk Sultanate of Egypt and North Africa. Cairo became a centre of the coffee trade, with coffeehouses springing up around the Azhar University. From there, we know that coffee and coffeehouses spread to Syria, particularly Damascus and the northern city of Aleppo. By the middle of the sixteenth century, coffeehouses were opening in Istanbul, the capital of the Ottoman Empire, which had conquered the Mamluk Sultanate in 1517. It is widely believed that the first coffeehouse in Istanbul was opened in 1555 in the commercial district of the city by two Syrian merchants: one from Aleppo, the other from Damascus.

There are two crucial things to consider during coffee's expansion. The first is that while coffee itself was spreading, the cultivation of coffee was not. As far as we know, all

coffee at that time was cultivated in Yemen and then either exported overland on well-established trade routes, or by sea through the western port of Mocha. Interestingly, although Ethiopia is widely acknowledged as the birthplace of coffee, it seems to have played no role in this, its first commercialisation.

The second important aspect was the culture of coffee, which went hand in hand with the coffee itself. While the consumption of coffee doubtless started in (and spread via) religious institutions, it also had a place in wider society, as witnessed by the rise of the coffeehouse. It must be remembered that since Islam forbade alcohol, there was no equivalent of the European tavern. It seems that coffee fulfilled more than just a desire for the drink itself; it filled a social need as well, providing a public space where men of all social strata could meet and socialise.

In so doing, it transformed the way that society interacted, aiding the spread of news and ideas. This, in turn, led to several backlashes against the coffeehouse, as the authorities, worried by the upheaval in the social order, tried to ban them. As we will see later, all of these bans were short-lived and quickly overturned. The march of coffee and the coffeehouse continued unabated.

COFFEE REACHES EUROPE

THE COFFEEHOUSE had become a staple of Islamic society by the mid-sixteenth century. Its spread westwards into Europe a century later owed much to simple trade, although war and conquest also played a part.

Staking a claim to be home to Europe's first coffeehouse is Malta. In 1565, the Great Siege of Malta took place, when the invading Ottoman Empire was repelled by the Knights of St John. A number of the invaders were captured and held as slaves, where they continued their practice of making and drinking coffee.

Trade must have played a role here since it is unlikely that the captured soldiers had an infinite supply of coffee with them. Malta, in the centre of the Mediterranean, was well placed to trade with the Ottoman Empire to the east, hostilities notwithstanding. The drinking of coffee spread beyond the Turkish prisoners into Maltese high society, and from there into the general population, with coffeehouses opening across Malta. Certainly by the late seventeenth century, coffee was well established in Malta, although still inextricably linked to the Turks. Writing in 1663, a German traveller, Gustav Sommerfeldt, noted 'the ability and industriousness with which the Turkish prisoners earn some money, especially by preparing coffee'. Meanwhile, in his book, *Virtu del Kafé*, published in Rome in 1671, Domenico Magri cites the Turks of Malta as the 'most skilful makers of this concoction [coffee]'.

What's clear is that from the late sixteenth century onwards, European merchants and travellers were increasingly coming into contact with coffee during their expeditions to the Ottoman Empire. In 1573, a German physician and botanist, Leonhard Rauwolf from Augsburg, made a trip to Tripoli, in modern Lebanon, before going on to Aleppo, Baghdad and Mosul, returning via Jerusalem in 1576. He is credited with being the first European to describe coffee, when the following description was published in 1583:

> They have a very good drink, by them called *chaube* [coffee] that is almost as black as ink and very good in illness, especially of the stomach; of this they drink in the morning early in the open places before everybody, without any fear or regard, out of China cups, as hot as they can; they put it often to their lips, but drink little at a time, and let it go round as they sip.

Another physician-botanist, the Venetian Prospero Alpini, travelled to Egypt in 1580. His work *De Medicina*

Egyptiorum, published in 1591, contains the first account of an actual coffee tree. Unsurprisingly it is Venice, another major trading centre with links to the eastern Mediterranean, which has a strong claim to hosting mainland Europe's first coffeehouse, which opened in 1645, although coffee itself had been traded at least 30 years before that, being used mainly for medicinal purposes.

London was not far behind, with its first coffeehouse opened in St Michael's Alley in 1652 by Pasqua Rosée, the Greek servant of a British merchant, Daniel Edwards, who lived for a while in Smyrna on the Aegean coast of Anatolia. Pasqua reputedly brewed the best coffee in the Ottoman Empire, which was 'black as hell, strong as death, sweet as love' according to a well-known Turkish saying. Pasqua introduced his master to the delights of coffee, and when Edwards returned to London in 1650, he brought both coffee and Pasqua back with him.

The coffeehouse was an immediate hit in London, with Pasqua serving 600 bowls of coffee a day within a few months of opening. It is not clear what happened to Pasqua, with the last record of him appearing in 1659, at which point he had opened two more coffee shops. Just four years later, in 1663, there were 82 coffeehouses within the Roman walls of the City of London, and by 1700 there were over 3,000 coffeehouses in London.

This pattern was repeated throughout Europe as coffeehouses were established in large trading cities. However, war and conflict still played a role in the spread of the drink, and it should be remembered that throughout the seventeenth century, the Ottoman Empire was periodically in conflict with Christian Europe. A crucial moment came in 1683 with the Battle of Vienna, which lifted a two-month siege of the city by the Ottoman army and is often seen as a turning point in the conflict, securing Europe's eastern borders against the Ottoman Empire.

A widely believed story is that the first coffeehouse in Vienna was established in the aftermath of the battle. In an echo of the coming of coffee to Malta, one of the defenders of the city, a Polish nobleman, Jerzy Franciszek Kulczycki, found a large supply of coffee in an abandoned Ottoman encampment, using it to set up the city's first coffeehouse.

In truth, however, the evidence all points to Vienna's first coffeehouse being established two years later in 1685 by an Armenian, Johannes Theodat.

By the end of the seventeenth century, the coffeehouse had become firmly established in European culture, just as it had in the previous century in Islamic society. Next, we will take a closer look at the culture of the coffeehouse.

THE RISE OF
THE COFFEEHOUSE

ALTHOUGH EUROPEAN and Islamic differed dramatically, their coffeehouse cultures were remarkably similar, taking as a model the coffeehouses first established in Cairo, which reached their peak in Istanbul.

Opinions vary on the quality of coffee in this period. Matthew Green, in *The Lost World of the London Coffeehouse*, quotes various descriptions of coffee, such as 'syrup of soot and the essence of old shoes'. Other tasting notes, which you won't see on any modern coffee packaging, included 'oil, ink, soot, mud, damp and shit'. Written in 1674, *The Women's Petition Against Coffee* (not exactly an unbiased source) described coffee as 'base, black, thick, nasty, bitter, stinking, nauseous puddle water'.

An equally biased source, Pasqua Rosée, who opened London's first coffeehouse, wrote a pamphlet, *The Vertue of the Coffee Drink*, which hailed coffee as a cure for just about every ailment, although he doesn't actually describe its taste.

The Vertue of the *COFFEE* Drink.

First publiquely made and fold in England, by *Pafqua Rofee.*

THE Grain or Berry called *Coffee*, groweth upon little Trees, only in the *Deferts of Arabia.*

It is brought from thence, and drunk generally throughout all the Grand Seigniors Dominions.

It is a fimple innocent thing, compofed into a Drink, by being dryed in an Oven, and ground to Powder, and boiled up with Spring water, and about half a pint of it to be drunk, fafting an hour before, and not Eating an hour after, and to be taken as hot as pofsibly can be endured; the which will never fetch the skin off the mouth, or raife any Blifters, by reafon of that Heat.

The Turks drink at meals and other times, is ufually *Water*, and their Dyet confifts much of *Fruit*; the *Crudities* whereof are very much corrected by this Drink.

Th   iality of this Drink is cold and Dry; and though it be a
n   neither *heats*, nor *inflames* more then *hot Poffet.*

          th the Orifice of the Stomack, and fortifies the heat with
               good to help digeftion. and therefore of great ufe to be
                    a Clocka   oo   n the morning.

                         ens the *Spirits*, and makes the Heart *Lightfome.*
          g   fore Eys, and the better if you hold your Head o-
     , an   ne Steem that way.

It fuppreffeth Fumes exceedingly, and therefore good againft the *Head-ach*, and will very much ftop any *Defluxion of Rheums*, that diftil from the *Head* upon the *Stomack*, and fo prevent and help *Confumptions*, and the *Cough of the Lungs.*

It is excellent to prevent and cure the *Dropfy*, *Goat*, and *Scurvy.*

It is known by experience to be better then any other Drying Drink for *People in years*, or *Children* that have any *running humors* upon them, as *the Kings Evil.* &c.

It is very good to prevent *Mif-carryings in Child-bearing Women.*

It is a moft excellent Remedy againft the *Spleen*, *Hypocondriack Winds*, or the like.

It will prevent *Drowfinefs*, and make one fit for bufines, if one have occafion to *Watch*; and therefore you are not to Drink of it *after Supper*, unlefs you intend to be *watchful*, for it will hinder fleep for 3 or 4 hours.

It is obferved that in Turkey, where this is generally drunk, that they are not trobled with the Stone, Gout, Dropfie, or Scurvey, and that their skins are exceeding cleer and white.

It is neither Laxative nor *Reftringent.*

Made and Sold in St. *Michaels Alley* in *Cornhill*, by *Pafqua Rofee*, at the Signe of his own Head.

The good news is that we can largely recreate the taste of early coffee. I tried a sample made by Jeremy Challender of a modern-day London coffeehouse, Prufrock, on Leather Lane. Jeremy was using a coffee from the Yirgacheffe region of Ethiopia, although I suspect it was roasted far lighter than a typical seventeenth-century coffee would have been. I have to say I rather enjoyed my seventeenth-century coffee, although you had to be wary of getting a mouthful of coffee grounds along the way. Matthew Green also makes his own version of seventeenth-century coffee, which was memorably described by the food critic Jay Rayner as 'disgusting', 'appalling', and something 'you could creosote fences with'.

Coffeehouses offered other attractions beyond the drink itself. Al Jazari, who we met earlier, cited an early sixteenth-century Arabic poem commonly titled 'In Praise of Coffee', which includes the line: 'Coffee is our gold. Wherever it is served, one enjoys the society of the noblest and most generous men.'[2] The opportunity for companionship, more than the coffee itself, seems to be at the heart of the rise of the coffeehouse. As an old Turkish saying goes, 'Not the coffee, nor the coffeehouse, is the longing of the soul. A friend is what the soul longs for; coffee is just the excuse.'

The phenomenon of people coming together over coffee is still with us today. When someone says 'let's go for coffee', do they really mean coffee, or is it an excuse for a catch-up? Of course, we also say 'let's go for a drink', where alcohol takes the place of coffee, but this does not apply in Islamic society, which had no equivalent of the tavern until the coffeehouse came along, partly explaining its meteoric rise.

In contrast, seventeenth-century London had taverns aplenty, which competed with the coffeehouses. Even so, it was the very lack of alcohol that was instrumental in the success of the coffeehouse, as Matthew Green argues. In London at that time, clean sources of drinking water were in short supply. Most people favoured watered-down beer and, as a result, were in a permanent state of mild inebriation. In contrast, the coffeehouse ushered in an era of sobriety, which went hand in hand with the coffeehouse's role in the exchange of information.

This was directly inherited from the Islamic coffeehouse, where people of all classes could mix freely, discussing politics and exchanging news. Early illustrations of London coffeehouses show long communal tables, crowded with men (no respectable woman would be found in a coffeehouse in seventeenth-century London). According to Green, conversation with strangers was positively encouraged. New customers would be greeted with the cry of 'What news have you?' or, more formally, 'Your servant, sir, what news from Tripoli?'

This role in the dissemination of news was noted by Samuel Pepys, writing in his diary on 19 October 1663. Describing his first visit to a coffeehouse in Cornhill, he

The Coffee-house Politicians.

notes that there was 'Much talk about the proceedings of the Turks. We hear that the plague has got to Amsterdam, brought by a ship from Algiers; it has also reached Hamburg.'

London's coffeehouse boom was followed by the relaxing of the laws on censorship, leading to a multiplicity of newspapers, something noted by visiting Swiss noble César de Saussure in 1726, who described finding gazettes and other publications in London coffeehouses: 'Workmen habitually begin the day by going to coffee-rooms to read the latest news. I've often seen shoeblacks and other persons of that class club together to purchase a farthing paper.'

The reputation of coffeehouses as sources of knowledge was such that they became known as 'penny universities', because the price of admission was one penny (the cost of a bowl of coffee). However, this reputation for being a place of exchange of information and open debate was also a source of considerable problems for the coffeehouse, as we'll see next.

THE SUPPRESSION OF
THE COFFEEHOUSE

WE HAVE tracked the spread of coffee and the subsequent rise of the coffeehouse in cultures as diverse as the Islamic Ottoman Empire and Christian Europe in the second half of the seventeenth century. But coffee's progress has hardly been smooth. Wherever coffee and coffeehouses sprang up, there have been those who sought to ban them, often with short-lived success.

The first recorded ban occurred in 1511 in Mecca, then part of the Egyptian Mamluk Sultanate. Various scholars argued that coffee was harmful, causing, among other things, leprosy. Since, under Islamic law, it is forbidden to consume anything that harms you, Mecca's governor, Hayir Bey, had plenty of grounds to outlaw coffee. It is possible that Hayir Bey's real motivation was political rather than religious; he feared that social unrest was fermenting in coffeehouses, where people met to discuss, among other things, Hayir Bey's unfitness to rule.

Whatever the reasons, the ban was short-lived. The sultan in Cairo, on learning of the ban, swiftly overturned it, his own physicians arguing that coffee was harmless. Again, it is likely that the motivation was as much political (and economic) as religious. Cairo was already the centre of a large and burgeoning coffee trade, which brought the Sultanate plenty of income from taxes. A ban, therefore, would have been economically damaging.

Despite this, it seems that the distrust of coffee amongst some groups of Islamic scholars never entirely went away. Over the next century, various attempts were made to ban coffee, some more successful than others. The next major ban came with the reign of Murad IV, although his motives seem more political than religious. He was 11 years old when he took the throne in 1623, only really taking control in 1632. A series of autocratic moves followed, designed to establish his absolute power and quell corruption and dissent. This included banning coffee, alcohol and tobacco, under threat of execution.

Ironically, given that the ban included alcohol, it seems that Murad IV was a habitual drinker who died from alcohol poisoning at the age of 27 in early 1640. The ban, however, did not die with him, although subsequent rulers relaxed the severe penalties, and slowly coffee returned to the mainstream of society. Indeed, it appears that despite various bans imposed in the Ottoman Empire, coffee-drinking continued in one form or another. Much like the prohibition of alcohol in America in the early twentieth century, bans on coffee merely drove it underground.

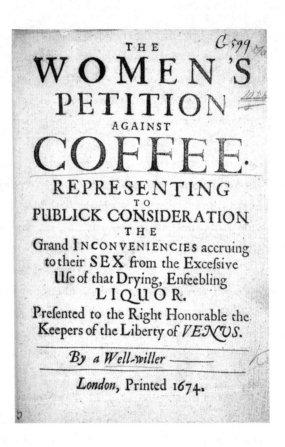

THE
WOMEN'S
PETITION
AGAINST
COFFEE.

REPRESENTING
TO
PUBLICK CONSIDERATION
THE
Grand INCONVENIENCIES accruing
to their SEX from the Excessive
Use of that Drying, Enfeebling
LIQUOR.

Presented to the Right Honorable the
Keepers of the Liberty of VENUS.

By a Well-willer ————

London, Printed 1674.

Islam was not the only religion to have issues with coffee. Its great rival, Christianity, also had cause to mistrust coffee, although ironically this was largely down to its association with Islam. One expert on the subject, Abdul-Rehman Malik, tells the story of Pope Clement VIII, who died in 1605.[3]

Towards the end of the Pope's life, Catholic priests argued that coffee was Satan's drink. Satan, they said, having forbidden his disciples (the Muslims) to drink wine, since it was sanctified by Christ, gave them coffee ('this infernal black beverage') as compensation. Debate raged about whether the Church should call for a ban on coffee and the Pope was asked to adjudicate. This prompted him to try coffee for himself, at which point he is reputed to have declared: 'This Devil's drink is so delicious, we should cheat the Devil by baptising it and making it a truly Christian beverage.'

Other opposition was on a more pragmatic level. Not long after London's first coffeehouse opened in 1652, local tavern keepers tried to have coffeehouses banned, fearful of the competition they provided. There was also opposition from women, who were excluded from coffeehouses. This led to *The Women's Petition Against Coffee*, published in 1674. It railed against:

> Excessive use of that Newfangled, Abominable, Heathenish Liquor called COFFEE, which ... has so *Eunucht* our Husbands, and Cripple our more kind *Gallants*, that they are become as *Impotent* as Age.

It also takes aim at the reputation of coffeehouses as sources of gossip:

Men by frequenting these *Stygian Tap-houses* will usurp on our Prerogative of *tattling*, and soon learn to exceed us in *Talkativeness*: a Quality wherein our Sex has ever Claimed preheminence: For here like so many *Frogs* in a *puddle*, they sup muddy water, and murmur insignificant notes till half a dozen of them *out-babble* an equal number of us at a *Gossipping*.

It ends with a call that the drinking of coffee 'may on severe penalties be forbidden to all Persons under the Age of *Threescore*'.

How seriously this was taken is not clear, but a year later, King Charles II, fearful of the potential of coffeehouses to promote sedition, attempted to ban them by royal proclamation. The proclamation was made on 29 December, but never actually came into force. Scheduled to take effect on 10 January, it was withdrawn on 8 January in the face of widespread public opposition.

ESCAPE FROM ARABIA

As WE have seen, coffee originated in Ethiopia, where it grew wild, before spreading to Yemen, where it was first cultivated. Then, over a period of two centuries, coffee and coffee culture expanded across the Ottoman Empire and into Europe. However, this expansion was purely in terms of green coffee as a traded commodity. During this time, coffee was cultivated exclusively in Yemen.

Surprisingly, Ethiopia, the birthplace of coffee, seems to have played no role in its early commercialisation. It seems likely that coffee was still growing wild in Ethiopia and continued to be consumed on a small scale, but there was no attempt to turn it into a commercial crop. Coffee trees were also found in other parts of the Ottoman Empire. For example, as we saw earlier, the Venetian Prospero Alpini published an account of a coffee tree he saw on a visit to Egypt in 1580, but there is no evidence that coffee was grown commercially there.

In contrast, coffee cultivation and export thrived in Yemen. The rulers of Yemen – first the Mamluk Sultanate and subsequently the Ottoman Empire – knew the value of the coffee trade and of their monopoly over it. Therefore, the export of live coffee trees and seeds was forbidden on pain of death. However, it was only a matter of time before coffee trees, and the knowledge of how to cultivate them, leaked out.

India, surprisingly, lays claim to be the first region outside Yemen/Ethiopia to grow coffee. A legend tells of an Indian Sufi, Baba Budan, who returned from the Hajj (the annual pilgrimage to Mecca) with seven coffee seeds taped to his stomach. These survived the trip and he successfully cultivated them in the hills around Mysore, in the modern-day Indian state of Karnataka.

Although it sounds appealing, I am inclined to discount this story simply as a legend. Coffee has undoubtedly been grown in Karnataka for a long time (and the state currently accounts for 50% of Indian coffee production), but its origins are probably far more prosaic and instead down to the activities of the Dutch East India Company (known by its Dutch initials as the VOC).

The VOC was established as a chartered company in 1602, partly as a reaction to the British East India Company, which dates from 1600. It was set up to exploit the spice trade, which the Dutch monopolised at the time. It impacts on our story because of the activities of Pieter van den Broecke, a VOC merchant who was sent to Arabia in 1614 as part of early attempts to expand the Company's trade networks.

It seems he was very successful, establishing a permanent settlement in the Yemeni port of Mocha on the Red Sea, at that time a major exporter of coffee.

There are various accounts of Van den Broecke's exploits, most of which claim that he smuggled live coffee plants back to the Netherlands, although there is no evidence that he obtained his cargo illegally. However he came by his coffee trees, no-one was particularly excited by their arrival in Europe in 1616. They were planted in greenhouses in Amsterdam where, by all accounts, they thrived, but it was not for another 40 years that the VOC began the commercial exploitation of its newly acquired coffee trees.

If this seems an unreasonably long delay, then remember that for the first half of the seventeenth century, coffee in Europe was a rare commodity. Only as the first coffeehouses were established did the trade in coffee take off. Moreover, the VOC had nowhere to cultivate coffee: to this day, coffee does not grow in Europe.

In 1658, the VOC began conquering Portuguese territories in Sri Lanka. By 1659, the Portuguese had been expelled from the island's coastal regions, allowing the VOC to establish a monopoly on the cinnamon trade. In order to secure this monopoly, the VOC went on to conquer Portuguese possessions on the southwest coast of India, in the modern-day state of Kerala (which neighbours Karnataka).

It seems that the VOC then brought the descendants of Van den Broecke's coffee trees to plantations, first in Sri Lanka and then in India, where they began to grow coffee on a commercial basis.

This was the first large-scale cultivation of coffee outside Yemen, and represents the beginning of the spread of coffee cultivation around the world.

COFFEE SPREADS
AROUND THE WORLD

ONCE THE genie was out of the bag, coffee began to spread in a band across the tropical regions of the globe, favouring regions at higher altitude. Although this band covers a large area of the planet's land mass, coffee generally followed the spread of European commercial ambitions.

This started in 1699 when the VOC sent coffee seeds from Indian plantations to its possessions in Indonesia, specifically to Java, from where it spread to other VOC possessions in the region. Within 15 years, these plantations were shipping coffee back to the European market and before long, the VOC was the dominant player in the European coffee trade.

This had a devastating effect on the coffee trade back in Yemen, which in 1634 had gained its independence from the Ottoman Empire. For the rest of the century, Yemen's economy flourished, buoyed by income from the growing coffee trade. With the arrival of coffee from Indonesia, however, demand for Yemeni coffee quickly collapsed. Part of the problem was competition, but there simply was not the capacity to meet high demand, with coffee-growing in Yemen dominated by small farmers producing coffee alongside subsistence crops. Over a period of 20 years, the economy crumbled and, by 1740, Yemen was no longer a major player in the international coffee trade.

It would be wrong to think that all was plain sailing for the VOC. Over-supply, causing disastrous drops in the price of coffee, plagued the VOC's coffee plantations, leading to the closure of its less profitable coffee-growing operations in India and Sri Lanka, forcing it to focus instead on its Indonesian holdings.

Despite these setbacks, the VOC dominated the coffee trade until about 1780. Ironically, the seeds of its downfall were planted by the Dutch themselves, when the mayor of Amsterdam gave a coffee tree (imported from one of the Java plantations) to the French King Louis XIV in 1714. Like the Dutch before them, the French at first seemed unaware of the commercial potential of the gift, instead planting it in the royal botanical gardens in Paris.

In 1723 a French officer, Gabriel-Mathieu de Clieu, who was stationed in the French possession of Martinique in the Caribbean, returned to Paris on leave. He was convinced that coffee would thrive in Martinique's tropical climate and decided that he would take a coffee plant back with him.[4] De Clieu tells of a heroic voyage with his precious cargo, surviving an attempted theft, an attack by corsairs off the coast of Tunis, an Atlantic storm and, finally, a period of calm lasting over a month. This was by far the worst trial according to

CH. EMONTS.

de Clieu. Supplies of drinking water were almost exhausted, and de Clieu claims that he had to share his meagre ration with the coffee tree in order to keep it alive.

He and the coffee tree made it to Martinique, where it was planted in de Clieu's garden, producing its first crop of cherries in 1726, which de Clieu used to plant trees around the island, leading to a second crop. There was one more twist to the tale: at that time, Martinique was principally given over to the cultivation of cocoa. Two years after the second harvest, de Clieu refers to 'horrible tempests accompanied by an inundation', which wiped out the cocoa plantations, allowing the natives to plant coffee trees instead.

Within a few years, the first commercial coffee plantations in the western hemisphere were well established, and de Clieu was able to send coffee seeds or trees to other French colonies in the Caribbean, including Saint-Domingue (present-day Haiti) and Guadeloupe.[5]

Coffee production in the Caribbean thrived. By 1777, there may have been over 18 million coffee trees in Martinique alone, and by 1788, French production in the Caribbean had eclipsed the VOC in Indonesia. Coffee was a truly global commodity, although it was destined for even greater things.

THE RISE OF BRAZIL

WE HAVE seen how the Dutch VOC in Indonesia eclipsed the coffee-growers in Yemen in the first part of the eighteenth century, while French plantations in the Caribbean took over the dominant position from the VOC in the later part of the century. This pattern was repeated in the early nineteenth century, when Brazil came from nowhere to dominate the world coffee trade – a status it retains today.

Although the rise of Brazilian coffee is essentially a nineteenth-century story, its roots go back to 1727. Much is made in popular histories of coffee of the smuggling of coffee plants leading to its spread around the world. We have already encountered various versions of this story. Such accounts appeal to the romantic in me, but in reality the global spread of coffee has much more to do with hard-nosed commercialism – and so it is with the introduction of coffee to Brazil.

Popular accounts tell a tale of Portuguese envy and seduction. The Portuguese, unable to obtain coffee seeds from legitimate sources in neighbouring French Guiana, instead sent one Francisco de Melo Palheta on a diplomatic mission, with the secret aim of acquiring coffee seeds. According to the story, he seduced the governor's wife, who gave him a parting gift of a bouquet which concealed several coffee cuttings and fertile seeds.

What these accounts fail to mention is that the initial plantations, in the northern Brazilian state of Pará, were a commercial failure. Multiple attempts were made to introduce coffee production to Brazil, with one of the more successful being credited to João Alberto Castelo Branco, who introduced coffee plants to Rio de Janeiro in 1760. Some claim that these plants were descendants of those in the north of Brazil, but others suggest they came from the Portuguese city of Goa in western India.

In the early nineteenth century coffee production in Brazil really began to take off, expanding southwards along the coastal states. In the 1820s, sugar and cotton accounted for 50% of the value of Brazilian exports, with coffee contributing less than 20%. In 1822, Brazil gained independence from the Portuguese and, in the following decade, sugar and cotton fell to about one-third of total exports, while coffee accounted for over 40%.

By the second half of the nineteenth century, Brazil was the world's leading producer of coffee, a position it has yet to relinquish. By this time, coffee production had spread throughout the Caribbean and across Central and Southern America, from Mexico to Peru and Bolivia. The British,

who were late among the European trading nations to the coffee party, started growing coffee on a large scale in India and Sri Lanka during the first half of the nineteenth century. Meanwhile, in the second half of the century, coffee was introduced to Central Africa. At the start of the twentieth century, coffee came full circle as the British introduced large-scale cultivation to East Africa, its natural home.

Although I have painted a fairly positive picture of the spread of coffee production across the globe, driven by commercial concerns, it would be remiss not to mention

43

coffee's dark side: slavery. The simple fact is that coffee production (in common with other crops, such as sugar, cotton and tobacco) would not have been possible without slavery. This is not a story of small-scale farmers, growing coffee by choice, but of large, foreign-owned plantations totally reliant on slave labour. Even in post-independence Brazil, the coffee boom of the mid-1800s was built on slave labour. Even where coffee was farmed without slave labour, the industry was organised to ensure that profit accrued to colonial powers rather than the local population.

We will see later how much this has changed, but for now we will return to the role of coffee consumption as an agent of social change.

THE RISE AND FALL OF
COFFEE IN BRITAIN

COFFEE'S SPREAD as a global crop enabled its consumption to move from being a rare luxury towards an everyday occurrence. But this was not an inevitable march towards global dominance, and in fact the rise of coffee culture was subject to many setbacks.

The success of the London coffeehouse, for example, proved to be short-lived. According to Matthew Green, the city boasted between 1,000 and 8,000 coffeehouses at the start of the eighteenth century. In contrast, Amsterdam, the hub of the European coffee trade, could muster just 32.

Green argues that coffee, in taking over from ale as the drink of choice, triggered a dawn of sobriety that laid the foundations for Britain's spectacular economic growth in the late seventeenth century. The London coffee-house brought people together, inspiring brilliant ideas and discoveries. For example, the first stocks and shares may have been traded in Jonathan's Coffeehouse, near the Royal Exchange, while merchants, ship owners and their captains gathered at the nearby Lloyd's Coffeehouse, witnessing the birth of the insurance industry.

These early developments in turn gave rise to financial concepts such as credit and securities, as well as providing the markets that allowed the dramatic expansion of Britain's network of global trade in Asia, Africa and America.

Ironically, given the role of coffee and the coffeehouse in developing international trade, the British were not major players in the actual business of coffee cultivation. It was only in 1796, when the British seized control of the coastal areas of Sri Lanka from the Dutch, that they started serious coffee cultivation. By 1815, the British had conquered the entire island and coffee production increased dramatically.

In 1869, however, the island was struck by coffee rust, a fungus that causes defoliation of a coffee tree, significantly reducing the yield of berries. Within ten years, the productivity of the Sri Lankan plantations had declined so much that they were no longer economically viable.

The second irony is that by this time, coffee had long since been surpassed as the drink of choice in Britain itself. Instead, it had been replaced by tea, one of the principal imports of the East India Company, which was bringing in tea from China. Its first shipment, which arrived in 1669, was of just 143lb (about 65kg), but this trade rapidly expanded, driven in part by Princess Catherine of Braganza, who married King Charles II in 1662. Tea was the new queen's drink of choice, which led to its adoption in high society. It may also have increased its appeal to women, who were largely excluded from coffeehouses.

However, this does not explain the rapid expansion of tea-drinking, which spread to all classes of society. Between 1720 and 1750, the East India Company quadrupled its imports of tea and by 1766, six million pounds of tea was being shipped from the port city of Canton by British vessels.

Counter-intuitively perhaps, some historians argue that it was the decline of the coffeehouse which prompted the increase in tea-drinking, rather than the rise of tea which prompted the decline in coffee.

Following this argument, the coffeehouse was the source of its own downfall. Its exclusiveness, and especially its exclusion of women, made coffee something that was not drunk at home. By the early 1700s, the coffeehouse had lost its novelty and, some argue, snobbery led the once-famed penny universities, accessible to all, to become the enclave of the few. All of this led to a decline in coffee-drinking.

In contrast to coffee, tea was easier to make. All that was required was boiling water. Coffee, meanwhile, required first roasting and then grinding, both of which needed to be done at home. Tea was also cheaper. In particular, since the British played no large-scale role in coffee cultivation or trade, which was controlled by their rivals (first the Dutch and then the French), it made sense to favour the tea trade, which brought in significant revenue.

So when coffee production was wiped out in Sri Lanka at the end of the nineteenth century, the British seized a great commercial opportunity, replacing coffee with tea plantations, first in Sri Lanka and then in India, reducing their reliance on imports from China.

However, by then, as we shall see, the British love of tea had proved instrumental in the rise of the American love of coffee.

THE BOSTON TEA PARTY

THE RISE of the coffeehouse also gave rise to social and political spaces where dissent was common. This was not just an Old World phenomenon; it spread to the New World, particularly to the new colonies in North America.

Coffee may first have been imported into the American colonies as early as the first decade of the seventeenth century, but the first records of coffee in America are from 1668, where there is a reference to coffee in New York. This was closely followed by Massachusetts, where Dorothy Jones was granted a licence in 1670 to sell 'coffee and cuchaletto [cocoa]'.

Coffeehouses, based on the European model, soon followed. However, with the British domination of the new colonies, coffee was never as popular as tea, which had overtaken coffee in Britain in the eighteenth century. Americans were also partial to the other British staple, beer. Despite this, coffeehouses played much the same socio-political role as they did in Europe, with the Colony of New York holding some of its General Assembly meetings in coffeehouses.

As moves towards American independence gathered pace, it is thought that revolutionary meetings took place in coffeehouses in Philadelphia, New York and Boston. Indeed, it was the revolution that thrust coffee into the limelight as the national drink of the newly independent nation.

One of the many complaints of the colonists was a tax on tea, which was imposed by the British government in 1767 as part of the Townshend Revenue Act. This was deeply unpopular in the colonies, which reacted with boycotts of all British goods and an increase in the smuggling of tea. The Townshend taxes were repealed in 1770, with the exception of the tax on tea, which remained at three pence per pound.

This defused the row for a little while, but things came to a head in 1773, when the British government passed the Tea Act, giving the East India Company a monopoly on the import of tea into the American colonies. While this actually led to a reduction in the price of tea, the colonists were unhappy with a range of matters, including the tax (which was incorporated into the Tea Act) and the attempt by the British government to impose a monopoly supply on the colonies. This led to the famous Boston Tea Party, when, on 16 December 1773, protestors boarded three trading vessels docked in Boston and dumped their cargo of tea overboard.

Tea rapidly became a symbol of the British, and as the positions of both sides hardened, colonists once again boycotted tea. Writing to his wife Abigail on 6 July 1774, the leading revolutionary John Adams related this incident:

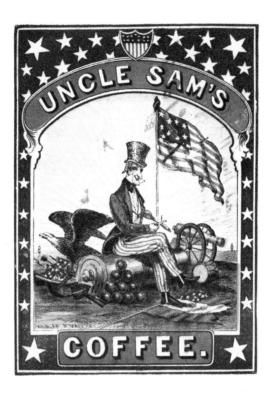

'Madam' said I to Mrs Huston, 'is it lawful for a weary Traveller to refresh himself with a Dish of Tea provided it has been honestly smuggled, or paid no Duties?'

'No sir', said she, 'we have renounced all Tea in this Place. I cant make Tea, but I'le make you Coffee.' Accordingly I have drank Coffee every Afternoon since, and have borne it very well. Tea must be universally renounced. I must be weaned, and the sooner, the better.

From then on, coffee was firmly associated with ideas of patriotism and slowly replaced tea as the nation's favoured drink. As America expanded westwards, its ever-increasing population led to a growth in demand for coffee. This increase in demand played no small part in the rise of Brazil as the world's leading coffee producer, with coffee flooding into America's eastern ports, such as New York, from where it was shipped across the country.

Increasing demand led to increasing commercialisation and, eventually, mass production. Coffee completed its journey from being a rare, exotic commodity, with small quantities of green beans being roasted in a pan over an open flame (the method originally used in Ethiopia) to being something commonplace, produced and traded on an industrial scale.

Similar revolutions were taking place in Europe, with coffee going from something that was freshly roasted, either at home or in the coffeehouse, to a product that could be bought from the grocery store. Large companies sprang up to the meet the demand, brands came to dominate, and coffee lost its mystique.

THE NINETEENTH-CENTURY COFFEE BOOM

SO FAR, we have traced coffee's spread to the point where it went global at the end of the eighteenth century. The stage was set for a boom in both coffee production and consumption, driven, in no small part, by the expansion of the American market. Europe (apart from Britain) played its part, with the coffeehouse becoming an established part of everyday society, although some estimates put average consumption by Europeans at around one-sixth of their American counterparts in the late nineteenth century. Despite relatively low levels, coffee-drinking took a firm hold in Europe, particularly in the north of the continent.[6]

Part of the problem that hindered coffee's rapid expansion in the eighteenth century was taxation. Although the cost of production was falling, European governments and their colonial offshoots saw coffee as a valuable source of income, imposing high taxation. This kept coffee as a luxury product.

All that changed in the United States, where coffee duties fell through the nineteenth century. From a high of 10 cents

BLICK VOM CAFE HEINRICHHOF
AUF DAS K·K·HOFOPERNTHEATER

per pound in 1812, coffee duty was cut to 5 cents in 1814 and then abolished in 1832. There was a blip during the Civil War when a duty of 4 cents was reintroduced, but the conflict also helped cement coffee's popularity, with the drink playing an important role in maintaining the morale of Union soldiers. This gave them a taste for coffee which carried over into civilian life after the war.

All this helped fuel a rapid take-up in coffee-drinking, with consumption rising from a minuscule ounce per person in 1783 to 13 pounds a head at the end of the nineteenth century. Coupled with this massive growth in consumption was a similarly impressive fifteen-fold rise in population, which grew from 5.3 million in 1800 to 76.1 million in 1900. On the back of this massive American growth, global coffee consumption also experienced a fifteen-fold increase in the nineteenth century, with America accounting for 40% of the world's coffee consumption at the start of the twentieth century.[7]

Of course, this rapid growth in consumption would not have been possible without a rapid growth in production. As we have seen, Brazil rose from nowhere to dominate world coffee production in the nineteenth century, its rise going hand in hand with the rapid expansion of coffee consumption, particularly in America. By the middle of the century, Brazil was producing more coffee than the rest of the world put together and, by the start of the twentieth century, 80% of the world's coffee came from Brazil.

This growth was by now decoupled from the rise of the coffeehouse, with coffee-drinking moving firmly into the home as prices fell and availability rose. Hand-roasting can produce great-tasting coffee (with guaranteed freshness!), but it's very time-consuming, ill-suited to anything but the small scale. In the nineteenth century, all this changed as technology revolutionised coffee roasting.

Although there were small-scale roasters which could be used at home as an alternative to the frying pan, the early nineteenth century saw various patents awarded for large, commercial roasters. In 1833, the first commercial roaster was imported into America from Europe, and before long there was a thriving commercial roasting market. American innovations soon followed, including the Carter 'pull-out' roaster, patented in Boston in 1846. This involved a rotating drum inside a brick oven or furnace, which was manually pulled out to be emptied when roasting was complete.

The next innovation came in 1864, when Jabez Burns was granted a patent in New York. His contribution was a roaster which self-emptied, simply by opening a door in the roasting drum. This allowed it to remain in the furnace, improving the efficiency of the whole process. Indeed, many modern roasters don't look that different from Burns's original model.

Within a few years, his roasters were in use across the country, but it was another innovation – the invention, in 1862, of a cheap, lightweight durable paper bag for the sale of peanuts – that changed the face of coffee. A Pittsburgh grocer, John Arbuckle, bought one of the first Burns roasters and started selling roasted coffee by the pound in the new paper bags. The business was so successful that before long, 50 people were employed to pack and label the coffee, with Arbuckle eventually going on to acquire an automated packing machine that did the work of 500.

During the American Civil War, New York became the major port for the importation of coffee, overtaking New Orleans, which had been blocked by the Union side. In 1871, Arbuckle moved to Brooklyn, establishing a factory that occupied a dozen blocks at its peak, roasting, packing and dispatching coffee across America.[8]

By the end of the nineteenth century, brands such as Arbuckle's were starting to dominate the American market, with similar developments taking place in Europe. Coffee had moved from the small-scale to the industrial and the next big revolution was on its way.

THE BIRTH OF ESPRESSO

FOR CENTURIES, nothing much had changed in the making of coffee: beans were ground just before use, often with a pestle and mortar, although variations on the spice mill had been around since at least the seventeenth century. On a larger scale, millstones, similar to those used for grain, were used. Meanwhile, preparing coffee involved nothing more complex than pouring hot water over the grounds and letting them steep. The final step was to encourage the grounds to settle, a practice that was aided in the early nineteenth century with various questionable additives, including eggs and fish oil.

Technology started to come into play with various European inventions, including the percolator (invented in Paris in 1806) and syphon (Berlin, 1830s). It is surprising how recent some common methods of coffee preparation are, again with the Europeans taking the lead. The pour-over coffee cone, using a paper filter, was patented in 1909 in Germany by Melitta Bentz, while the cafetière or French press was only patented in 1929 (ironically, given the name,

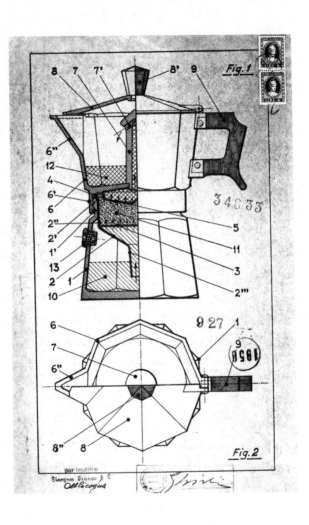

Fig. 1

Fig. 2

by an Italian, Attilio Calimani). It was another Italian, Luigi De Ponti, who patented the moka pot or stove-top espresso machine in 1933. In contrast, the humble ibrik (also known as the cezve or briki) appears to have been in use since the fifteenth century!

While these were all designed for home use, the problem facing the coffeehouse was how to make coffee in volume. This could be addressed by making large pots of coffee, although this was far from ideal, as anyone who has had coffee from a pot left standing on a hotplate for too long can readily attest to. The alternative is making individual cups of coffee, but this takes time: the methods described above, as well as not having been invented at the start of the twentieth century (with the exception of the ibrik), all take around four to five minutes to make a single cup. What was needed was something that could quickly make an individual cup of coffee.

Step forward the espresso machine.

The roots of espresso go back to the late nineteenth century, and, like many of this book's stories, this one is full of stops and starts. In 1884, Angelo Moriondo of Turin was granted a patent for 'new steam machinery for the economic and instantaneous confection of coffee beverage'. The main drawback of Moriondo's invention was that it was a bulk-brewer. It was also a commercial failure, with Moriondo only making a few hand-built models.

All this changed in 1901 when Luigi Bezzerra invented a machine capable of making individual cups of coffee. He was unable to capitalise on his invention, and his patents were purchased by Desiderio Pavoni. In 1906, with Bezzerra's continued involvement, Pavoni's Milan workshop started producing commercial espresso machines.

These early models relied on a boiler producing steam at pressure, which was then forced through a densely packed puck of ground coffee. This introduced many elements common to the modern espresso machine, including the individual group head (where the water is expelled under pressure) and the portafilter (which holds the ground coffee and attaches to the group head). These early machines could make an individual cup of coffee in under a minute and, by virtue of employing multiple group heads, a single machine could make 1,000 cups an hour.

Despite their early success, these machines had their drawbacks. Boilers were heated with open flames, making them difficult to control, although electric heating elements, introduced in the early twentieth century, helped alleviate that. The main issue was the pressure: by relying purely on steam pressure, these early machines could manage, at most, two bars of pressure (that is, twice atmospheric pressure). In contrast, modern espresso machines use nine bars, but for that, we need to wait until the late 1940s, and another Italian invention.

Milan's Achille Gaggia is credited with inventing the modern lever espresso machine. Gaggia's great breakthrough was to use a compressed spring to force the water through the coffee under high pressure. In Gaggia's design, the boiler only has to heat the water, which is delivered to a small chamber. A lever is then pulled down, which compresses the spring. On release, the spring forces the hot water out of the chamber and through the ground coffee.

With far greater pressures, extraction occurred much more quickly, with a lever machine capable of making an espresso in around 15 seconds. Extractions were also more consistent, although pulling the lever required considerable effort, something which was alleviated by the next breakthrough in 1961, when Ernesto Valente introduced the world to the iconic Faema E61. The key was replacing the spring in the lever machine with a motorised pump to deliver the water at pressure.

Many see the E61 as the basis of the modern espresso machine, although lever machines are still being manufactured today and have many faithful adherents. Regardless, the scene was now set for the modern espresso revolution.

THE ITALIANS AND
POST-WAR LONDON

THE INVENTION of the espresso machine meant that individual cups of coffee could be prepared, on demand, for customers. This soon caught on in Italy, but it took a while to spread around Europe and the rest of the world.

The most notable espresso bar boom occurred in London during the 1950s and 1960s. Post-war London was in many ways a drab place. Food rationing only ended in 1954 and the city was rebuilding after the devastation of the war. Rents were cheap, particularly in less fashionable parts of London such as Soho; people's disposable incomes were growing; and there was a newly emerging youth culture.

It was this environment in which an itinerant Italian dental-equipment salesman, Pino Riservato, found himself. Appalled by the quality of the city's coffee (often made from chicory and coffee essence) and missing the espresso bars of home, Riservato decided to do something about it. In 1953, he opened the Moka Bar, London's first espresso bar, in what had been a bomb-damaged laundrette at 29 Frith Street in Soho.

Riservato was related to a director of Gaggia, enabling him to obtain a concession to import Gaggia machines into the UK. The country's first experience of the gleaming, steaming Gaggia was therefore at the Moka Bar, which was intended to showcase the Gaggia as much as anything else.

The Moka Bar proved to be an immediate success, and was soon followed by a host of others. Despite our modern taste for chains, brand identities and cookie-cutter stores, these early espresso bars did not set out to imitate the Moka Bar in either look or feel. Instead, a host of independent operators moved into the market, each catering to a particular clientele.

Often they had little experience in the catering trade and virtually no experience in coffee. Still, the entry requirements were low. Stores were available at very low rents, and apart from the cost of the espresso machine, which was the major capital outlay, they could be fitted out cheaply. Moreover, since they did not serve alcohol, an expensive licence wasn't required, although most found that to make ends meet, they needed to stay open late into the evening and serve food rather than just coffee.

The Moka Bar and its ilk quickly made their mark on popular culture. By 1956, the popular radio comedy *Hancock's Half Hour* had an episode, 'Espresso Bar', in which the show's star, Tony Hancock, opens an espresso bar. This picked up on the amateur nature of the business, with Hancock proclaiming:

> That's the vogue these days, find yourself a dirty old cellar, get a couple of barrels and a long plank, candles in bottles and you're in business.

Back in Soho, iconic espresso bars soon sprang up, such as Le Macabre at 23 Meard Street, which was a horror-themed café where you could sit in a coffin to drink your coffee. In a similar vein, Heaven and HELL opened in 1955 with a white-walled upstairs (Heaven) and a black-walled basement, accessed via a doorway painted as a giant devil's mouth (Hell).

A year later, 2i's Coffee Bar opened next to Heaven and HELL at 59 Old Compton Street. Now famed as the birthplace of British rock and roll, it played a large part in cementing the link between the espresso bar and the rise of youth culture. Too young to drink in pubs and with little else catering for them, teenagers flocked to espresso bars like 2i's, where some of the UK's best-known names cut their teeth on the cramped stage in the basement. Of course, back then they were not well known, with the likes of Harry Webb (Cliff Richard) and Thomas Hicke (Tommy Steele) starting their careers there.

The new espresso bars catered to all tastes, such as the Partisan Coffee House at 7 Carlisle Street. Opened in 1958 by historian Raphael Samuel, it drew a left-wing political crowd. However, it seems it took its socialist principles too far and closed in 1962, unable to make ends meet.

Although other espresso bars were more successful, the boom as a whole was short-lived. 2i's, for example, closed in 1970, and by the mid-70s, the boom was over. At its height, London alone had over 500 espresso bars, none of which (to my knowledge) has survived to the present day. It is uncertain why the espresso bar was unable to become a permanent feature of British life, but from the mid-60s, they faced stiff competition for the youth market, with night-clubs and dedicated music venues taking over.

These days, there is very little left of Soho's espresso bar revolution. If you want to recreate something of the atmosphere, the closest you will come is Bar Italia on 22 Frith Street, not far from the site of the Moka Bar. Established in 1948, it both pre-dated the espresso bar boom and outlasted it. There is still a lever espresso machine behind the bar, one of the oldest in London, although if you want to see London's oldest working espresso machine, check out Doctor Espresso Caffetteria by Putney Bridge Station, where you'll find a 1950s Gaggia Tipo America, lovingly restored by Doctor Espresso himself, Russell Kerr.

FRIENDS AND THE RISE OF THE MODERN COFFEE SHOP

BY THE TIME I really started to notice coffee, in the early 1980s, coffee in the UK largely meant instant coffee, and coffee shops were practically non-existent. There were cafés, but these were often rather grand affairs, where you went as much for the cake as for the coffee (or tea). Back then, the height of coffee sophistication was filter coffee, usually made in a cheap, electric brewer, using pre-ground beans. I remember friends buying coffee from Taylors of Harrogate and my being seduced by the wonderful aromas, the starting point of my love affair with coffee.

I tasted my first espresso in 1989 on a trip to Spain. I remember being distinctly unimpressed, considering it akin to crude oil, a thick, black sludge. It wasn't until my first trip to Rome in 2000 that I really began to understand, and have a passion for, espresso.

However, while the 1950s espresso bar boom in London was largely Italian-inspired, what follows owes much to American popular culture.

In 1971, Starbucks was founded in Seattle in the Pacific Northwest. Initially selling beans, the owners became inspired after a trip to San Francisco, where they visited Peet's, another iconic name in American coffee, although less well known abroad. This led to Starbucks making coffee as well as selling beans, although back then, it was all filter coffee. The real revolution came when Howard Schultz, the newly installed head of marketing, went to Milan in 1983 and discovered Italian espresso bar culture.

It was Schultz, who bought Starbucks in 1987, who turned it into what it is today, a primarily espresso-based, multi-national coffee shop chain. Starbucks' growth was spectacular, from six Seattle stores in 1987, to 55 in 1989, based in the Pacific Northwest and in Chicago, where the first store had opened just two years earlier. Store numbers almost tripled by 1992 and again by 1994, when there were 425 Starbucks across the USA. By 1996, Starbucks had grown to over 1,000 stores, including one in Tokyo.

Back in the UK, things were moving much more slowly. That began to change with the sitcom *Friends*, which aired in the US from 1994 to 2004, arriving in the UK in 1995. A large part of *Friends* centred on Central Perk, a coffee shop in the West Village in New York, where one of the characters worked as a waitress and the others would gather. *Friends* made the coffee shop seem a welcoming place, a cool place, a place that people wanted to be.

Soon the coffee shop scene was taking off in the UK, with home-grown chains such as Costa and Coffee Republic opening branches around the country. Another major player at the time was the Seattle Coffee Company, founded in 1995 by a married couple, Scott and Ally Svenson, who had moved to London and missed their daily dose of Starbucks. By 1998, they had 64 stores, mostly in London, which is when Starbucks came knocking at their door, wanting a foothold in the British (and European) market. The Svensons sold up, Starbucks moved in, and the rest is history.

Since then, the growth of the coffee shop chains has been spectacular. At the end of 2015, the market leader was Costa, with over 1,500 stores around the country. Starbucks, in comparison, had just over 700, with Caffè Nero coming in third with 500. Although chains such as Costa and Nero sell themselves with a firm nod towards Italian coffee culture, their actual cafes, in terms of layout, service and product, are firmly in the American model made wildly successful by Starbucks.

It was Starbucks which coined the phrase 'third place' to describe the coffee shop, somewhere beyond work and home where people could gather informally, much as they did in *Friends*. These days, of course, people also use coffee shops as places to work, with the laptop and smartphone generation using them as mobile offices. In part this has sustained the coffee shop boom in the UK through two major recessions, and the growth in the market shows no signs of slowing down.

THE COFFEE TRADE

LET'S TURN to the state of coffee today and where we might be going in the future.

We'll start with the claim from the introduction that coffee is one of the world's most traded products, second only to oil. This, as we've known for many years, isn't true. It's one of those zombie statistics that refuses to die, quoted by so many people that everyone assumes it's true. No lesser figure than Mark Pendergrast, author of the highly regarded *Uncommon Grounds*, made this mistake. In the introduction to the first edition (published in 1999) he said coffee was the 'second most valuable exported legal commodity on earth (after oil)', an error which he later corrected, writing several articles on the subject.

This myth is so widespread that it is worth asking about its origins. The most likely explanation is a misquoting of data from the United Nations Conference on Trade and Development. These go back to the 1970s and rank the value of commodity exports from developing economies, putting coffee second only to (you've guessed it) crude oil.

So where does coffee rank in world trade? The second edition of *Uncommon Grounds* puts coffee as the world's fourth most valuable *agricultural* commodity (my emphasis), although, of course, in a world of fluctuating prices, the answer very much depends on when you ask the question. Whichever way you look at it, coffee is a valuable commodity, providing livelihoods for millions of people around the world.

A common figure is that there are 25 million coffee farmers around the world, while Pendergrast suggests that five times that number, 125 million, rely on coffee for their livelihood. While this includes the barista in your local coffee shop, the vast majority live and work in the coffee-growing regions of the world. Coffee is a labour-intensive business, one which has relied in the past on slavery. Although that's behind us now, in many parts of the world, those working in the coffee industry, often undertaking seasonal work such as coffee harvesting, still live in poverty.

Their output is staggering. According to the International Coffee Organisation (ICO)'s latest figures, coffee production has been relatively stable over the last five years, with around 150 million 60 kg bags of coffee being produced in 58 countries (equivalent to 9 million tonnes of coffee). However, this relative stability masks the fact that global coffee production has increased by around 50% in the last 25 years.

The majority of this coffee is consumed in Europe and North America. The top 35 coffee-importing countries account for 120 million bags a year, a figure which has increased roughly in line with production over the last 25 years. Naturally, you would assume that this would leave 30 million bags to be consumed in the coffee-growing countries, but actual consumption is 50 million bags, a figure which has been steadily increasing, more than doubling in 25 years.

So how does that work, exactly? Well, coffee has a relatively long shelf life: not all the coffee traded in a given year was grown in that year. In fact, in the 1990s, global stocks totalled over 50 million bags, compared to annual production of around 100 million bags. It's only in the last 10 years that stocks have been falling, reaching a low of 15 million bags in 2016/17.

The top five producers account for almost three-quarters of global production, with Brazil leading the way with 55 million bags, or just over one-third of global production. The big surprise is second-placed Vietnam, which in 2016/17 produced 25 million bags, or 17% of the global total, but which was languishing in 17th place in 1990 with a mere 1.4%. Third place is Colombia (10% of global production), while Indonesia is fourth and Ethiopia, the birthplace of coffee, is fifth, accounting for just over 4% of global production.

Top dog when it comes to importing is the USA, accounting for 28 million bags, almost one-quarter of global imports. However, this is dwarfed by the European Union, which taken as a whole imports over 60% of the world's coffee, led by Germany at 21 million bags. As with coffee growers, five countries dominate the import market, accounting for almost two-thirds of coffee imports. Italy, unsurprisingly, is third, Japan a close fourth and France just behind in fifth. Between them, they account for another 24 million bags. In comparison, Brazil consumes 20 million bags, putting it just behind Germany's total imports.

Of course, figures can be misleading. Germany, for example, re-exports over half the coffee it imports in terms of roasted coffee and other products, thus consuming far less than Brazil. And, of course, the figures are heavily skewed by population. Finland and Norway, for example, who between them import less than 2% of the world's coffee, regularly top the per-capita consumption charts, while America rarely makes it into the top 10.

COFFEE, A GLOBAL CULTURE

COFFEE IS, by its very nature, a global product. Although predominantly grown in the tropical band around the equator, it is primarily consumed outside of the tropics, in the northern hemisphere. Coffee culture is also global, and has been from the start. Just looking at London, we have seen successive waves of influence over the last 400 years, from the Ottoman coffeehouses of Istanbul through the Italian espresso craze of the 1950s and the American influence of Starbucks at the turn of the millennium.

Coffee, and particularly speciality coffee, has been undergoing a boom in the last decade. Ten years ago, you could count the number of independent speciality coffee shops in London using your fingers. When I started my blog, *Brian's Coffee Spot*, in 2012, I rapidly became aware that I was at the start of a boom. From a handful of shops 10 years ago, London now has hundreds, supported by a bewildering array of small, independent coffee roasters. This boom isn't confined to London: it's happening all over the country. Brighton, Bristol, Edinburgh, Glasgow,

Manchester: all have growing, vibrant coffee scenes. Wherever I look, I find great coffee, made with passion.

So where did this come from? Much is home-grown, but there is an undeniable global influence, particularly from Australia and New Zealand (ironic, given that between them they account for less than 2% of world coffee imports). Around 10 years ago, Australians and New Zealanders, frustrated by what they perceived as a lack of good coffee in London (and the UK in general), decided to do something about it by setting up their own coffee shops, drawing heavily on their native café culture.

Many of the iconic names of the London coffee scene from the late 2000s are owned by Australians (Lantana, Kaffeine, Taylor Street Baristas) or New Zealanders (Flat White, Scooter Café). The same can be said of some of the big names in roasting, such as Nude Espresso, Allpress and Ozone, all of which had their roots in Australia/New Zealand.

It's not just the coffee that they brought, though. It was also a focus on food, a whole café culture that is the polar opposite of the US-based counter-service model. Here you took a seat and had your coffee (and food) brought to you rather than standing around by the counter while a barista hollered something approximating to your name. While brunch is often considered American, London's brunch boom in recent years owes as much to the Antipodean influence as anything else.

However, it would be wrong to overlook local contributions, just as it would be wrong to think that this was only happening in London. Pioneering roaster Monmouth celebrates its 30th birthday in 2018, while Union Hand-Roasted Coffee began roasting in 2001 and can now be found on the country's supermarket shelves while still remaining true to its micro-roaster roots. Elsewhere, Peter James in Ross-on-Wye formed James Gourmet in 1999 and Steve Leighton started roasting as Has Bean in 2003. Both are still going strong.

The influence hasn't been restricted to the Antipodeans. Around the world, people are exploring coffee and coffee culture. James Hoffman won both the UK and World Barista Championships in 2007, using a coffee roasted by Anette Moldvaer. Together they went on to form Square Mile Coffee Roasters in 2008, Anette bringing with her a lighter roasting style that was pioneered in Scandinavia and then gained popularity around the UK. This was in contrast to the darker, more Italian-influenced roasting style that dominated in Australia, New Zealand and America.

None of this is unique to the UK, nor is the influence one-way. Coffee culture is constantly reinventing and re-exporting itself. On recent trips to Hong Kong, China and Japan, all traditionally tea-drinking cultures, I found booming coffee scenes. In Hong Kong and China, coffee is seen as a specifically Western niche, with coffee shops that wouldn't look out of place in the UK, while the menus of poached eggs on toast and smashed avocado showed an Antipodean influence. Japan, meanwhile, has a more established coffee shop tradition which is merging with Western influences to produce its own unique style.

Nor are these simply aping cultures and styles. Rather they are often leading the way, with baristas from around the world competing in the annual World Barista Championships. Since 2007, when the UK's James Hoffman was crowned champion, the winners have come from Ireland, UK, USA (twice), El Salvador, Guatemala, Japan, Australia and Taiwan.

WHERE DO WE GO
FROM HERE?

I'll FINISH with that most foolish of activities, trying to guess the future. However you look at it, coffee is on the up. While global production figures vary markedly year on year, as climate and the global price of coffee influence the market, there's an undeniable upward trend. Figures from the ICO show that average production over the 10 years from 2008 to 2017 is a quarter higher than it was from 1998 to 2007. Average coffee imports have shown a similar growth, while internal consumption in coffee-growing countries has shot up by 50%.

Unfortunately, this growth in production does not seem to have been matched by a growth in the price paid to coffee farmers. The figures are more volatile and harder to compare, varying by country and type of coffee, but analysis by the ICO shows that although average prices have been rising, once corrected for inflation, prices are actually flat, while the costs of production are rising. What's worse, prices are volatile, making it very hard for coffee farmers to plan from year to year. For example, from April 2011 to November 2013, ICO figures show that nominal prices more than halved.

One of the ways forward for coffee farmers is to improve the quality of the coffee they grow. Although evidence is more anecdotal, there's been a dramatic increase in the demand for high-quality coffee. James Hoffman, the co-founder of London's Square Mile Coffee Roasters, observes that what I've called speciality coffee, defined by a focus on the coffee's tastes and origins, as well as the farmers who grew it, has boomed in the UK in the last 15 years. Recent figures estimate that 50% of speciality coffee shops and roasters in the UK have been trading for less than two years. Hoffman argues that this explosive growth is reaching a plateau, a point where excellent coffee becomes commonplace, and he expects this to lead to growth slowing down, along with a general consolidation.

Despite this generally rosy picture, the global coffee industry faces significant challenges, some of which are fundamental to coffee itself. Although there are many varietals (or subspecies) of coffee, often with markedly different flavour profiles, and while coffee is grown in about 60 countries around the globe, it's startling in its lack of genetic diversity. Of the coffee in production today, it is estimated that 70% is from a single species, *Coffea arabica* (more commonly known as Arabica), with all the different varietals being traced back to a single ancestor.

This makes coffee highly susceptible to disease. We saw an example of this earlier, when coffee leaf rust wiped out coffee production in Sri Lanka in the 1870s. Since then, this devastating disease has spread around the globe, reaching South and Central America in the 1970s and 80s. A coffee leaf rust epidemic in Central America in 2012 pushed coffee prices to an all-time high, and the disease remains a major threat to coffee production.

Partly to address the problem of disease, cultivation of another species, *Coffea canephora* (commonly known as Robusta), was introduced in the late nineteenth century. Robusta (as the name suggests) is more resistant to disease. It's also easier to care for, has higher yields, and grows at lower altitudes and over a wider range of climates than Arabica. This is important because Arabica is under threat from global climate change, and could lose many of its existing habitats as average global temperatures rise. A report by researchers at Kew Gardens in the UK, published in 2012, suggests that wild Arabica coffee (which grows in Ethiopia) could become extinct by 2080, while a 2016 report from Australia's Climate Institute suggests that we could see the amount of land available for commercial coffee production halved by 2050.

One solution is to grow more Robusta, which currently accounts for 30% of world coffee production, with Vietnam as the world's largest producer. However, compared to Arabica, it simply doesn't taste as good. Instead, scientists around the world are looking at breeding new varieties of coffee, combining Arabica's taste with Robusta's robustness.

None of this addresses a third challenge: simple economics. For coffee and coffee farming to be sustainable in the long term, it has to offer people careers. In an increasingly globalised market, there is a danger that the next generation will turn its back on coffee farming as a way of life, either turning to other, more profitable/stable crops, or simply leaving the land altogether as they find other opportunities.

Coffee farming is a long-term business. It's not as simple as planting a crop and harvesting it a few months later. Coffee trees take 3–5 years to reach maturity and produce fruit. Farmers also need the infrastructure (coffee mills, for example) to process the cherries into green coffee suitable for export. That is why the speciality coffee movement puts such an emphasis on building relationships with farmers, ensuring that they are paid a fair and stable price for their coffee, so that coffee farmers and, more importantly, their children, can see that they have a sustainable future.

So where do we go from here? The great fear is that we are living in a bubble, that in 20 years' time, we'll look back and think that this was a wonderful time to be in coffee. This is nothing new: London experienced the rise and fall of the coffeehouse from the mid-seventeenth to the mid-eighteenth century, and the even shorter-lived espresso craze of the 1950s and 60s.

Those cycles of boom and bust were driven by social factors, while coffee today faces other, more serious challenges that I've outlined here. So it's a distinct possibility that coffee's global dominance will be short-lived, going the way of London's early pioneers or the espresso bars of the 1950s.

All I can say is that I hope not. I have faith that we will rise to and overcome the challenges. And rest assured, as long as there are people in the world growing, roasting and serving excellent coffee, I'll be out there, finding places to drink it!

BUT DOESN'T ALL COFFEE TASTE THE SAME?

OVER THE last 25 years I've been on a very personal coffee journey. Twenty-five years ago is when I started to become a regular drinker of what I called back then 'proper coffee'. This marked my transition from exclusively drinking (very bad) instant coffee to starting to use whole coffee beans which I ground at home. I started with a cheap filter machine, but quickly moved to a cafetière (French press) since I felt the filter imparted an unpleasant taste to my coffee.

One of the problems facing coffee is the perception of taste. Let's be honest: we all know what coffee tastes like. It tastes like coffee: dark, bitter. You know, coffee-like. That's certainly how I thought 25 years ago. Sure, I knew that different preparation methods had an impact on the taste of the coffee (witness my switch to the cafetière) but that was about it.

Part of the problem is that we rarely taste just the coffee. Many people in Britain and America are drinkers of coffee and milk, be it in the modern form of a cappuccino, latte or on-trend flat white, or just plain old coffee with milk, which is how I used to drink my morning cafetière. Compare this to the experience of drinking wine. Rarely do we drink wine with anything added to it; we're just tasting the wine. With coffee, the taste is heavily influenced by the milk. Not that there's anything wrong with drinking coffee with milk. Indeed, the pairing of coffee with milk can produce some exquisite drinks.

Nevertheless, it heavily influences how we perceive the taste of coffee, sometimes masking it altogether. Long before I caught the speciality coffee bug, I would refer to the 'buckets of milk' approach adopted to coffee sizes by some of the national chains as 'coffee-flavoured milk drinks', acknowledging that it was primarily about the volume of milk, not the coffee.

Back at home, I would take my coffee with a splash of milk, but, in a foreshadowing of things to come, if I had really good-quality coffee, I would drink it black. I was also developing a taste for espresso, something which I viewed almost as a different drink.

My appreciation of coffee took a radical turn when, five years ago, I began writing my blog, *Brian's Coffee Spot*. I vividly remember my first taste of what I would come to know as speciality coffee in a coffee shop in Bristol. I had a Guatemalan coffee from a farm called Finca el Platanillo, made with a device called a Clever Dripper (which I described at the time as a 'fancy cafetière'). At the barista's suggestion, I had it black, and my first thought on seeing the coffee was that it looked like tea. I was similarly unimpressed with the taste, writing that 'the subtle flavours that these brewing methods seek to extract from the beans are not what I'm looking for in my coffee. Indeed, the very things that they seek to exclude (the fines and the oils) are, I suspect, what makes a good coffee for me.'

How things have changed! Four years on, and it's precisely these subtle flavours that I seek out, both in coffee shops and at home. Do I want something bold and chocolatey? Or sweet and floral? Or bright and fruity? The variety in coffee, which I was once, if I'm honest, scared of, I now revel in. Along the way, I realised that I had spent 20 years making coffee I didn't like the taste of, then putting milk in it to make it palatable. These days, I understand that I can make coffee I do like the taste of, without needing to add anything to it.

BREWING COFFEE

WHEN IT comes down to it, brewing coffee is a relatively simple business. You just need a way to grind the beans, then add water which dissolves various chemical compounds in the coffee beans, including caffeine (a process known as extraction), and there you have it: coffee.

Coffee brewing can be divided into two basic categories which I'll call infusion and percolation, although, as we'll see, it's wise not to get too hung up on the terminology. Infusion involves pouring (hot) water onto coffee grounds, leaving them to brew, then separating the grounds from the brewed coffee. In contrast, percolation involves passing (hot) water through the coffee grounds. I say (hot) water, by the way, since both infusion and immersion techniques can be used with cold water, producing something known as cold brew, but we'll come to that.

Infusion is the original way of making coffee. The grounds were separated by letting them settle to the bottom of the cup, and this was how coffee was made for centuries until various technological innovations were made in the nineteenth century.

The first challenge is how to separate the coffee grounds from the brewed coffee, saving you from getting a mouthful of sludge with your coffee. The most common infusion method is the cafetière or French press, patented in 1929. This uses a metal mesh which is pushed down through the coffee, trapping the grounds at the bottom.

Another ancient method, which has been around for at least 500 years, and is still in use, pretty much unchanged, is the ibrik. In contrast to every other brewing method I know, where the water in contact with the coffee is either at a constant temperature, or drops through the brewing process, the water in the ibrik starts off cold and heats up throughout the process. That said, the ibrik is still an infusion method, where the coffee grounds are in contact with the water throughout the brewing process.

Other variations on the infusion method were devised in the nineteenth century, such as the syphon, which dates from the 1830s, which is when percolation came to the fore, with the percolator having been invented in 1806. This involves passing hot water through a bed of ground coffee, but has the disadvantage that the extracted coffee can be mixed back in with the hot water and recycled through the coffee grounds. The moka pot (or stove-top espresso machine), invented in 1933, employs the same principles, but keeps the extracted coffee in a separate chamber at the top.

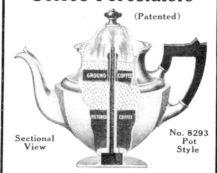

Both the percolator and moka pot use the pressure of water vapour to force the hot water through the coffee grounds. An alternative is the pour-over filter, which uses gravity. Water is poured onto the ground coffee which is held in a filter, fine enough to hold back the coffee grounds, but while still letting the water through. Original filters were made of linen and are still in use today, but the breakthrough came with the invention of the Melitta filter, with its paper filters.

All these methods are still in use today, although the percolator fell out of favour in the 1970s and 80s as electric filter machines made it onto the home market. Since then, there has been an explosion in different pour-over filters, many originating in Japan, where considerable thought has gone into the shape of the filter, how many holes it has, and whether the bottom is flat, ridge-shaped or a single hole. Similar innovation has come in the electric filter market, where the human pouring hot water on the grounds has been replaced by automatic boilers and shower heads. However, they are, in essence, the same method.

There are also hybrid methods such as the Clever Dripper, which uses gravity to draw the brewed coffee through a filter paper, and the Aeropress, in which the brewed coffee is pushed through a filter. Both, however, are at heart immersion brewers.

Espresso machines, by the way, are another variation of percolation, just a rather extreme one, with water forced at high pressure through the ground coffee. Modern pod-based machines are also, in essence, percolation methods, which pass hot water at pressure through the ground coffee.

This brings me neatly onto the factors affecting coffee brewing, namely grind size, water temperature, pressure and contact time. Put simply, the smaller the grind size and the higher the temperature/pressure, the more quickly extraction occurs. The more quickly the coffee is extracted, the shorter the contact time required. This is why espresso and pod machines can make coffee in tens of seconds: the coffee is ground extremely finely and the pressure is high, so extraction is fast. In contrast, a pour-over or cafetière might take four minutes. Here you have atmospheric pressure and a coarse grind. Finally, at the far end of the scale, cold brew, which uses cold water at atmospheric pressure, can take many hours.

You'll notice I have not mentioned instant coffee here, which is a little unfair, since it accounts for perhaps half the world's coffee consumption. Invented in 1881, it became increasingly popular during the twentieth century, providing a cheap and easy way for people to make coffee. Instant coffee is produced using pressurised liquid water, the resulting coffee then being dried to produce a powder or granules. Alternatively, a coffee concentrate can be produced by reducing the liquid. The main disadvantage with instant coffee is taste: it simply does not compare to freshly brewed coffee!

FURTHER READING

For more information on the contemporary coffee scene in particular, see the author's blog, Brian's Coffee Spot (http://brian-coffee-spot.com).

BOOKS, REPORTS AND ARTICLES

John Adams, Letter to Abigail Adams, 6 July 1774 http://www.masshist.org/publications/apde2/view?id=AFC01d090

Anonymous, *The Women's Petition Against Coffee* (1674)

The Climate Institute, 'A Brewing Storm: The Climate Change Risks to Coffee' (2016) http://www.climateinstitute.org.au/verve/_resources/TCI_A_Brewing_Storm_FINAL_WEB270916.pdf

Matthew Green, *The Lost World of the London Coffeehouse* (London: Idler Books, 2013)

James Hoffmann, *The World Atlas of Coffee* (London: Mitchell Beazley, 2014)

International Coffee Organization, 'Assessing the Economic Sustainability of Coffee Growing' (2016) http://www.ico.org/documents/cy2015-16/icc-117-6e-economic-sustainability.pdf

Anette Moldvaer, *Coffee Obsession* (London: Dorling Kindersley, 2014)

Mat North, *Coffee: A Modern Field Guide* (We Hunt & Gather, 2014)

Matthew Partington, 'The London Coffee Bar of the 1950s: Teenage Occupation of an Amateur Space?', in *Occupation: Negotiations with Constructed Space* (2009, conference paper, available online)

Mark Pendergrast, *Uncommon Grounds: The History of Coffee and How it Transformed the World* (New York: Basic Books, 2010)

Jimmy Stamp, 'The Long History of the Espresso Machine', *Smithsonian.com* (2012) http://www.smithsonianmag.com/arts-culture/the-long-history-of-the-espresso-machine-126012814/

Steven Topik, 'The World Coffee Market in the Eighteenth and Nineteenth Centuries, from Colonial to National Regimes', *Economic History Working Papers* (2004)

William H. Ukers, *All About Coffee* (New York: Tea and Coffee Trade Journal Co., 1922)

Maxwell Colonna-Dashwood, *The Coffee Dictionary* (London: Octopus, 2017)

WEBSITES

Food and Agriculture Organization of the United Nations http://www.fao.org/home/en/

International Coffee Organization http://www.ico.org/

The International Trade Centre http://www.intracen.org/
James Hoffmann's blog http://www.jimseven.com

RADIO PROGRAMMES

The following are all accessible online at time of writing.

The Long View, BBC Radio 4, 2014 http://www.bbc.co.uk/
    programmes/b04cf5pv
The Muhammadan Bean, BBC Radio 4, 2016 http://www.bbc.
    co.uk/programmes/b07tq8cd
Coffee and the God Shot, The Food Programme, BBC Radio 4,
    2016 http://www.bbc.co.uk/programmes/b07sxqt8

NOTES

1   In telling the following story I am indebted to the journalist Abdul-Rehman Malik and his excellent BBC Radio 4 documentary, 'The Muhammadan Bean' (2016), which links the spread of coffee to Islam.

2   Translation from William Harrison Ukers, *All About Coffee* (1922).

3   This section is indebted to 'The Muhammadan Bean' as above.

4   There is some argument about the date of his trip, some giving it as 1720, but in his own account, written shortly before his death at the age of 87 in 1774, de Clieu gives the year as 1723.

5   Some experts challenge this narrative. While not disputing that de Clieu introduced coffee to Martinique, they argue that coffee was being commercially grown in Saint-Domingue in 1715 and in the Dutch territory of Suriname in South America in 1718.

6   Even today, Finland tops the world rankings of per-capita coffee consumption, followed by Norway and the Netherlands, with Austria, Denmark, Germany and Belgium all in the top ten.

7 In contrast, America does not even make the top 20 in the modern-day per-capita rankings.

8 Long after the Arbuckle factory had closed down, one of its abandoned stable blocks became the home of the Brooklyn Roasting Company, which began roasting there in 2010.

LIST OF ILLUSTRATIONS

104

ACKNOWLEDGEMENTS

The Philosophy of Coffee would not have come about without Daniel C. Stevens, who generously put me forward as the author. It would also not have happened without the patience, support and excellent editing of Robert Davies at the British Library. I'd also like to thank Dr Matthew Green for being an (unwitting) inspiration and sometime role model.

On a personal level, this book is dedicated to my parents, Edward and Vera Williams, without whose unconditional support throughout my life I would never have achieved all that I have. It is also dedicated to Katie Giacomini, who, despite not drinking coffee, enthusiastically supported and encouraged me as each chapter rolled off the word processor.

Finally, I could not have written this book without the help and support of countless coffee shop owners, roasters, baristas and bloggers around the UK, who, over the last five years, have generously shared their time and knowledge with me over numerous cups of coffee.

Also available in this series

THE PHILOSOPHY OF
BEARDS
THOMAS S. GOWING

THE PHILOSOPHY OF
WINE
RUTH BALL

THE PHILOSOPHY OF
TEA
TONY GEBELY

THE PHILOSOPHY OF
GIN
JANE PEYTON

THE PHILOSOPHY OF
CHEESE
PATRICK McGUIGAN

THE PHILOSOPHY OF
BEER
JANE PEYTON

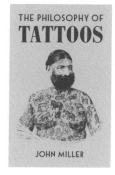

THE PHILOSOPHY OF
TATTOOS
JOHN MILLER

THE PHILOSOPHY OF
WHISKY
BILLY ABBOTT

THE PHILOSOPHY OF
CURRY
SEJAL SUKHADWALA
BRITISH LIBRARY